How to be an HG Hero!

Helping children understand Hyperemesis Gravidarum

By Caitlin Dean - Illustrations by Paul Colledge

To Joseph Miranda and Bo Briggs, HG Heroes - with love

Mummy has a teeny tiny baby growing in her tummy.

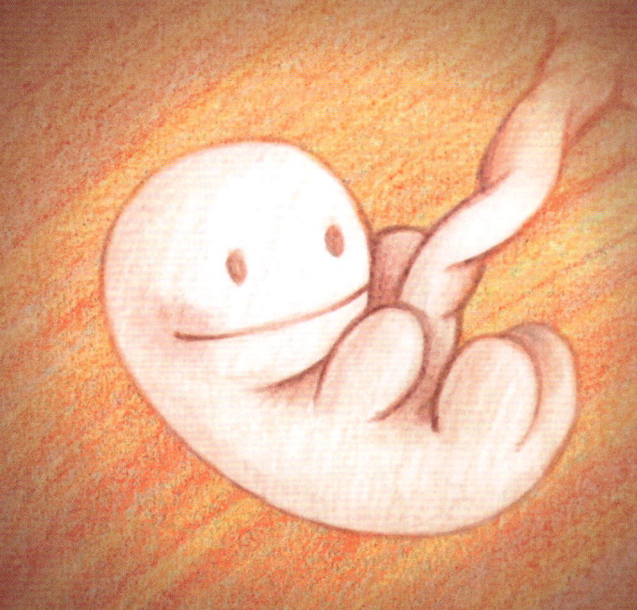

Some mummies get very sick when they have a baby in their tummy.

Some mummies have to see the doctor and take lots of medicine so they aren't so sick.

Some mummies have to go to hospital to have more medicine through a special needle in their hand or arm.

Sometimes this is called a drip.

If your mummy is one of these mummies it might make you feel sad.

Mummy might not be able to play with you or cuddle you when she is sick.

You might feel scared or worried and have lots of questions.

It's okay to ask questions and talk about how you feel.

Who will you talk to and ask all of your questions?

There are lots of things you can do to help mummy and daddy and be an **HG Hero!**

You can help by getting yourself dressed.

You can help by...

picking up your toys.

You can help by...

carefully fetching a drink of water for mummy.

What other HG Hero ways can you help around the house?

Putting your dirty clothes in the washing basket...

clearing the plates after dinner...

laying the table...

or making your bed.

It would probably help mummy if you try to be as quiet as a mouse when she is feeling very sick and resting.

Maybe you could look at some books or do some drawing?

As the baby gets bigger mummy will start to feel better some days.

She might be able to play with you again or go for a walk with you.

But some days she might still be very sick and need to rest a lot.

On those days you need to be a super helper for mummy again.

It may seem like a long time that mummy is sick but as each day passes...

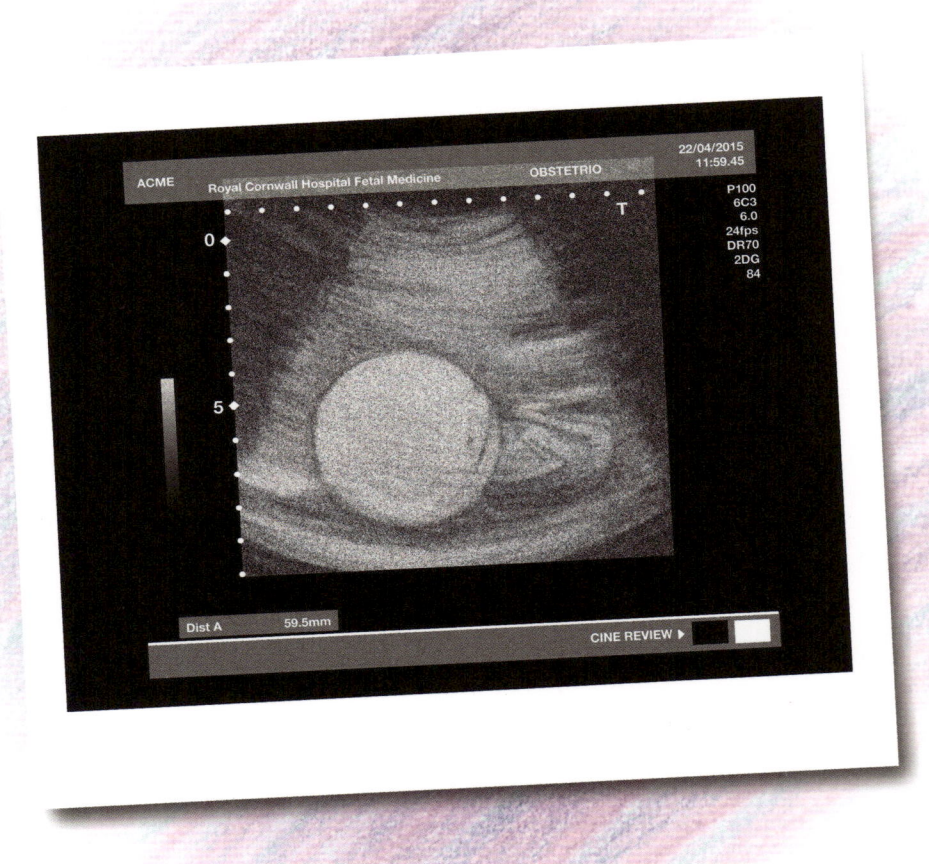

the baby gets bigger and closer to being born.

Until one day...

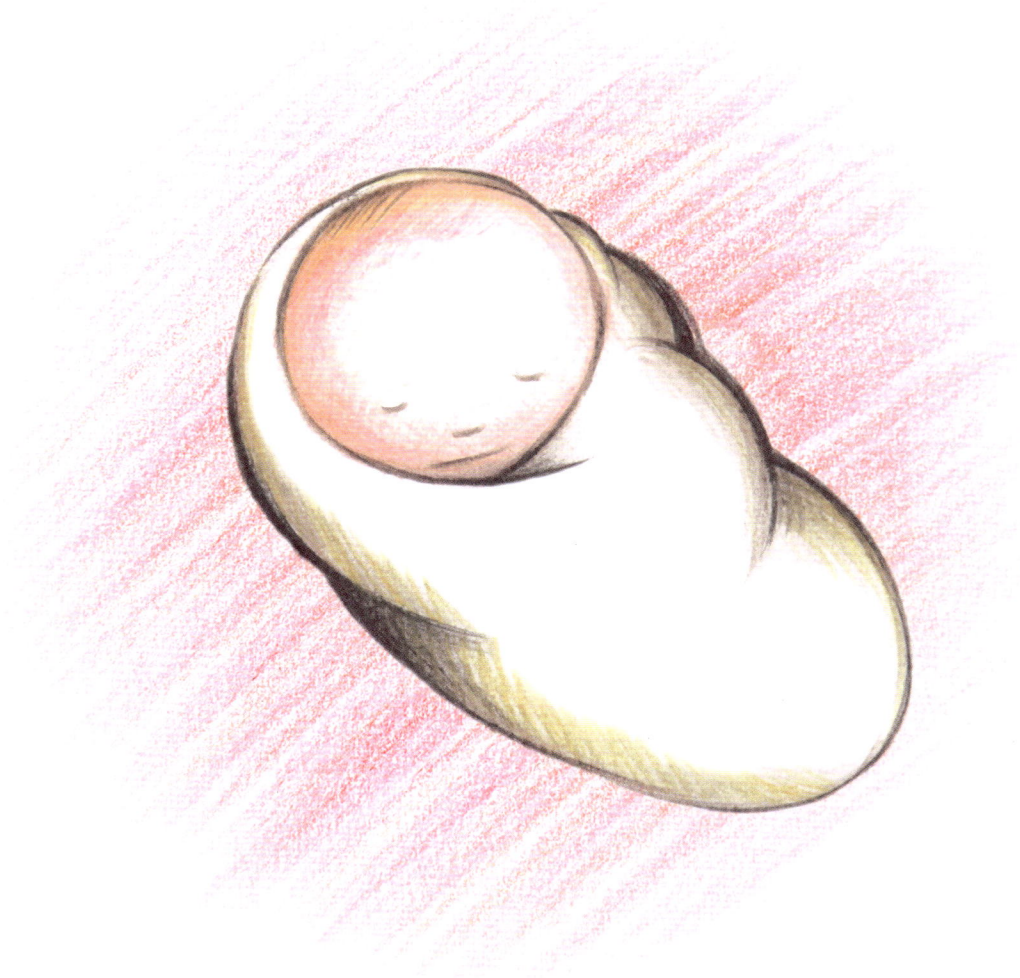

your baby brother or sister will arrive.

Mummy won't be sick any more...

and all that practice helping mummy means

you'll be the best big brother or sister around.

You'll be a true HG Hero!

Help and information for families affected by Hyperemesis Gravidarum (HG)

Suffering HG, as if not hard enough the first time round, can be even harder when you already have little ones at home to look after. Early effective treatment is key and there is a wealth of information available about treatments and support available online.

Please don't suffer alone… contact these people for support:

For UK and Ireland help and support contact **Pregnancy Sickness Support**:

Helpline 024 7638 2020

Website **www.pregnancysicknesssupport.org.uk**

For USA and international support contact the HER Foundation:

Website **www.helpher.org**

My Spewing Mummy blog can be found at **www.spewingmummy.co.uk** and my book, *Hyperemesis Gravidarum – The Definitive Guide*, contains a vast amount of information about the treatments, self-help, support, recovery, planning for another pregnancy and information for partners. It's available from high street retailers and online.

For a range of "HG friendly" activities for toddlers, maximum distraction for kids with minimum effort from mum, check out www.adventuresofadam.co.uk/hyperemesis-gravidarum

Copyright © Caitlin Dean 2015

Copyright © Illustrations and design by Paul Colledge

The right of Caitlin Dean to be identified as the author of this work has been asserted in accordance with the Copyright, Designs and Patents Act 1988. All rights reserved. No portion of this book, either text or illustrations, may be reproduced in and form, including electronically, without the express written permission of the author.

Permission can be obtained from **hello@spewingmummy.co.uk**

The Spewing Mummy brand and logo are the property of Caitlin Dean

ISBN: 978-0-9930623-2-2

1st edition, paperback

Published by Spewing Mummy in 2015

This certificate is awarded to:

For being a true HG Hero to:

Your support, compassion and care has made a massive difference while she was suffering hyperemesis gravidarum. This certificate is awarded by Spewing Mummy to show appreciation and raise awareness about how we can improve the experiences of women with hyperemesis.

Signed

This certificate is awarded to:

For being a true HG Hero to:

Your support, compassion and care has made a massive difference while she was suffering hyperemesis gravidarum.

This certificate is awarded by Spewing Mummy to show appreciation and raise awareness about how we can improve the experiences of women with hyperemesis.

Signed

spewing mummy